# HENRY M. BURTON

# Systems Thinking for Beginners

*Learn the essential systems thinking skills to navigate an increasingly complex world for effective problem solving and decision making*

First edition

This book was professionally typeset on Reedsy.
Find out more at reedsy.com

# Contents

# 1

# Introduction

Everyday life is filled with problems, and our success is often determined by how well we deal with them. No area of life is ever free of them: problems and complex situations at the workplace that make it difficult for us to reach our performance goals, a conflict with a family member or friend or romantic interest that makes the relationship difficult, an appliance or computer program that doesn't work as it should, sudden expenses that threaten our household budget, and the list goes on and on. Sometimes solutions present themselves fairly quickly, and we can rectify things and move on. But other times, the solution we reach for doesn't work so well – the same problems keep coming around again. Then we struggle to find any sort of approach.

We all could benefit from developing a "toolkit," a set of practices that we can use to deal with problems. This toolkit would help us get a handle on the world we live in, in all its facets: technical, professional, and personal. It would help us identify, diagnose, and address all the problem areas that challenge us. We could use it to get down to root causes, so we aren't distracted by surface symptoms and can find solutions that last – and maybe head off further problems down the road.

"Systems thinking" is one such toolkit. It has been used effectively by corporations, nonprofits, and government agencies around the world. Elements of system thinking were essential in the rise of successful businesses like Toyota. And it isn't just for big corporations. Systems thinking can be applied to global issues such as poverty and problems that are closer to your community, your social group, or your workplace. A word of caution is in order, however. Systems thinking isn't a magic wand; applying it takes understanding, patience, and courage. Systems thinking may cause you to question the assumptions that have motivated your choices in the past. You may find that a lasting solution to a vexing problem may make the situation worse for a while before it gets better. But when it is done right, it can be empowering.

Systems thinking begins with the insight that we are surrounded by interconnected systems, which is a fundamental shift from our tendency to see things in isolation. So just what is a "system"? For our purposes, a system is a group of related entities that work together to produce some desired result. They can take on many forms: your body can be a system. So can a company, or a family, or an assembly line, or an appliance. Systems can be broken down into subsystems: your body has many organs that hopefully work together to keep you healthy and active. A company can have many divisions – personnel, production, marketing – that work together to earn a profit. A machine can have hundreds of parts.

When things are going well, all the system parts work together in harmony, and we hardly even notice. We are more likely to notice a system when it is malfunctioning. When your computer crashes or your car doesn't start, that system will get our full attention. In fact, if we're relying on that system for something critical, we cannot ignore it. One breakdown on a subway line can mean hundreds of riders are late for their jobs or appointments. If the delay lasts long enough, they will need to find alternative ways - another system - to get where they are going.

Understanding systems, how to identify them, and how they really work internally is empowering because when there is a problem, you can act intelligently. When you recognize a system and learn how it functions, the causes and effects that work their way through the system, you can work within the system to achieve the results you want. In time you can anticipate breakdowns, allowing you to compensate in advance or head them off entirely. Understanding systems means you are less likely to find yourself fighting pointlessly against them. You can achieve more with less effort and frustration. Systems thinking can help you improve the systems that you deal with, and, as we are all surrounded by systems in all aspects of life, improve your life quality, personally and professionally.

This book will help you achieve that. It is written for anyone who wants to know more about systems thinking, what it is, and how to apply it. We will provide an overview of basic concepts, key principles, and common tools. We will give examples of common systems and stories about how problems developed and were solved by applying systems thinking. We will provide common scenarios and advice about how to deal with them and where to look for solutions. We will provide a list of resources at the end that you can look at to deepen your understanding.

In the first chapter, we will explain in more detail what "systems thinking" means and what differentiates it from more common ways of looking at the world around us. We will discuss how to identify a system and what is inside and outside the system. We will give some guidance as to when systems thinking is most likely to be useful.

In Chapter Two, we will talk more about systems thinking and the different levels of thinking about an event or a problem, starting from observing incidents to reassessing our basic assumptions about a system. We'll also introduce you to a basic but powerful systems thinking method, the "five whys."

In the Third Chapter, we talk more about how systems are identified and how they work. We will talk about connections within systems. Some are reinforcing, and others provide balance. These can lead to feedback loops. Feedback can be critical to how systems work and can lead to unexpected results when they aren't accounted for. We will move from there to talk about system boundaries: how to decide if something is or is not part of a system, the role of time in a system, and the "stocks and flows" of resources.

Chapter Four shows you various graphics used to illustrate how systems work. These include connection circles, behavior over time charts, causal loop graphics, and "stock and flow" charts.

The Fifth Chapter illustrates four common system thinking scenarios using charts and examples. We will show you a few ways that systems can break down and suggest ways to deal with each one.

The final chapter will discuss how you can apply systems thinking to problems in your own life and also to larger social issues.

# 2

# What is Systems Thinking?

To understand systems thinking, we have to begin by defining what exactly a system is.

> *A system is a set of interrelated entities, things, or people, that work together to produce a result.*

Systems can be man-made or natural. They can arise as a product of conscious design or natural development, or some combination of both.

A system is non-reducible. That means you cannot remove or hamper any part of a system without affecting other parts of the system and ultimately affecting the overall results. Or, to put it another way, the various parts of a system are interconnected.

Most people tend to start with the assumption that things they encounter are disconnected, that they operate more or less independently, and their functions are not related. We aren't completely blind to interrelation; we certainly recognize basic and clear relationships. We know it's likely to take us longer to drive to work during the rush hour because the heavy traffic will slow the highway system down. But as we go about our daily lives, there are relationships we don't really think about. As you walk past a tree, you probably don't think that your health and that of the tree are interrelated.

But in a very real sense, they are interrelated. Human beings, and all animals really, need oxygen in the air to breathe. Trees and other plants replenish that oxygen. And for your part, when you exhale, you release carbon dioxide that plants use to sustain themselves. This oxygen cycle takes place throughout the globe, and itself is a major part of the global climate. The oxygen cycle is a system that supports animal and plant life throughout the world. While your life probably wouldn't be dramatically affected if that one tree were pulled up, your ability to breathe is dependent upon millions of trees thriving. And those trees, in turn, depend on animal life.

Remove enough trees, and the system will be noticeably damaged: there's less oxygen circulating. Remove enough animals, and the system is damaged in the other direction; there's less carbon dioxide for the plant life to process.

Systems exist on far smaller scales than the global environment. Systems can be entirely mechanical, with no living components. For instance, your car (assuming you drive one) is a system made of many parts: wheels, engine, radiator, and so on. Of course, a living thing can be a system too. Or even a body part, like your hand. A system can also be social in nature, like a fan club. All these systems and subsystems, and the relationships between them, can get to be a little overwhelming. Whenever you apply systems thinking, you should understand and define the system's boundaries, as you will see in Chapter Three.

All systems have a purpose, either one that it was expressly designed for or perhaps one that people assign to them over time. Your car's purpose is to transport you to places you need or want to go. The purpose of your hand is to hold and manipulate things. The purpose of a fan club is to allow supporters of a sports team (or a musician or a band or an actor or an actress) to talk about their favorite players and maybe arrange trips to see them play.

Each of these systems needs all of its parts to work well. Your car has thousands of parts. Some of them are critical; your car would be useless without a working engine and could only go a few blocks with a flat tire. Even a minor part, such as the motor that raises and lowers one of the windows, will affect the car's performance if it goes out. The car will still be drive-able if the passenger-side window is stuck wide open, but the passenger compartment will be a lot less comfortable if it's cold or raining outside.

Likewise, with your hand, if you lose a finger, it will be weaker. You will find it more difficult to do a lot of things like writing or operating a can-opener. A good fan club needs all of its officers to do their jobs. If it loses a significant number of regular members, it will lose dues and volunteers to help with events.

Within these systems, there is an order: each part of the system has its particular role to play and frequently a specific location. A car's parts are designed specifically to perform their mechanical functions: the engine provides power to the transmission, which transfers that power to turn the wheels. The bones, muscles, and tendons are all set in specific locations so that the fingers and the thumb can move independently or together. A dislocated finger – a bone that is moved out of its regular joint – is painful.

And the officers of a fan club have their specific roles: the secretary keeps organizational notes, the treasurer minds the club's money, and the President directs the club's overall operations. There may also be informal roles: the President may ask one of the club's members to find tickets for an upcoming away game, while another member arranges transportation and finds a hotel.

A system will frequently use feedback to maintain its own stability. Systems have the means to adjust to change and/or repair the damage. When you hit the accelerator on your car, the system will push more fuel through the fuel injectors into the engine, so the car has the power it needs to pass another car or get itself rolling after stopping at a red light. Your hand can heal if it is cut or can mend a broken bone. And the fan club should have its own processes to maintain itself. If it is losing members, leadership should take note and either start a membership drive to bring in new people or reduce dues or plan new activities to keep current members on board.

So that's what we are talking about when we refer to a "system." "System thinking" means taking a holistic approach, keeping the entire system in mind when we need to address a problem or make a change. When we think and act with the whole system in mind, we are more likely to identify the root causes of problems and find lasting solutions. Whatever symptoms that troubled us before are less likely to come back. We are also less likely to encounter unintended consequences because we can see all the relationships within the system. Even if there are likely to be negative side-effects, we will know about them in advance and can be ready to deal with them.

Systems thinking is often contrasted with analytical thinking. Analytical thinking tends to break things down into their components. When confronted with a malfunctioning machine, the analytical thinker's first response is to take it apart and look at all the parts separately to get a picture of the machine's inner workings and understand its operations. The system thinker is more likely to observe the machine at work, see how its users operate the machine, and how it connects with all the other machines.[1]

Presented with an automobile to study, the analytical thinker will want to pop open the hood and strip parts away from the engine. The system thinker will be more likely to go for a ride and watch as the car moves through the streets. There's nothing necessarily wrong with either approach, but it's best if you can do both. There are things you can learn from watching a car in operation; observing the way it makes turns, accelerates, and brakes, noticing the environments it operates in, the way it moves through narrow residential streets and fast highways. You will not be able to deduce these from breaking down the parts.

Systems thinking is not a cure-all, and you shouldn't feel obligated to apply it to every situation you encounter. There will be times when the quickest approach, dealing with the symptoms and moving on, will be best. Suppose you wake up one morning with pain in your knee. In that case, you might want to treat your knee as a system (it would qualify as a system) and work through all the factors that might cause it to be sore – overly strenuous exercise or excess weight, for instance. Or you might take some pain medication and go on with your day. If this knee pain is an occasional thing and not too severe, then you're probably fine just taking the pill. However, if the pain is severe or you sense there is a pattern (even if you can't quite put your finger on the pattern), you might want to apply system thinking and try to get down to the root causes.

# 3

# Learn to Identify Systems

Every day we deal with minor inconveniences, unexpected situations, mundane activities, and occasionally pleasant surprises. The dog chews on your slippers. You get a phone call from a coworker asking where to find a file. A friend invites you to dinner. These are isolated events, and we treat them that way; we deal with them as they come, and we move on to the next thing.

But sometimes, there is more to an event than initially appears. System thinkers sometimes describe events as the tip of an iceberg. What we see above the water is just a small part of something larger. What we see is the relatively minor incident, but underneath that may be patterns that we should be noticing and systems we should be making ourselves familiar with. And beyond that may be assumptions that we might need to reconsider.[2]

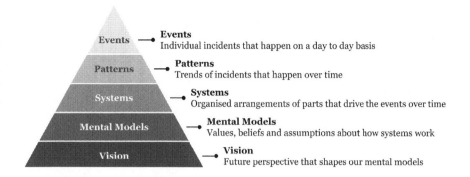

*Graph 01: Iceberg Model*

Suppose you're at your office and you're working with your computer. Up to now, this computer has served you well. You've had it for a couple of years, and it hasn't caused you any problems. So you're responding to an email or entering data into a spreadsheet, and the computer freezes on you. After a minute or so of waiting, you reboot and pick up whenever you last saved your file. Hopefully, it won't happen again. That is an **event**.

An hour or so later, your computer freezes again. That's twice in one day! The freeze-ups are starting to form a **pattern**. You may still believe the computer is pretty reliable, and you don't need to call tech support. Hopefully, this is just a coincidence, or it will clear up on its own. Still, you might begin to deal with the symptom by saving more often until the symptom goes away.

Or perhaps you start to think about your computer as a **system**. You almost certainly will after it locks up one or two more times. You probably aren't ready to ask for a new machine, but you suspect that there is something wrong that needs to be corrected. If you have some computer knowledge, you might start to think about the hardware or software inside your computer. Maybe a file is corrupted? Or there's a program you downloaded that isn't compatible?

11

Or there's a problem with the memory? You might call in a technician. This thing isn't going to go away on its own.

At this point, you are starting to engage in some system thinking. But that doesn't guarantee your problem will be solved immediately. If you and the technician are unable to find the problem, you will have to reconsider your **mental model** for the computer system. Up to now, you have assumed that the problem is a relatively minor one: a software glitch or a relatively inexpensive part that needs to be replaced. The computer is still basically reliable and up-to-date and should last five years as your last one did. Or so you think. But if this problem continues to go on, you will start to consider asking for a replacement. Maybe this thing just can't be fixed. Now you have called into question one of your assumptions from when this whole thing started.

Finally, you may learn from your coworkers that they are having problems with their computers too. And their problems may be larger in scope than yours. The network can't handle all the data they send in and out, and the software your company uses is behind that used by your clients and competitors. Someone might suggest replacing all the computers and servers with new equipment and installing new software. That is a **vision** for a replacement system that spans the entire office. Addressing the root cause might mean additional costs and effort in the short term, but it will benefit the company in the long term because staff will have equipment that does more for them with fewer breakdowns.

All that is what might lie underneath the surface the next time your computer malfunctions and you have to restart it!

Now, this doesn't mean you have to replace all the computer gear in your office the next time your desktop hangs up. Sometimes an event is just an event. The challenge is to identify when an event is part of a pattern, and the pattern points to systemic issues. If there is a *system* problem, whether it's a defective desktop or your entire office computer system is outdated and unable to do the job, the number and severity of problems will likely escalate. In that case, the sooner you and your team realize you have a systemic problem, the sooner you can start looking at the system, find the root of the problem, and address it. By applying system thinking, you can even anticipate and prepare for issues that might arise, head off problems before they start, and optimize your system to provide the results you want.

# The Five Whys

There is a practice that system thinkers sometimes apply when they identify a problem. It is called "The Five Whys." The basic principle is that you should begin by asking why an event happened. Then take the explanation, turn it around, treat it as a separate event and ask why that happened. Then take the second explanation, treat that as another event, and ask why that happened. Keep going until you have asked "why did that happen" five times. At that point, you should have gotten down to the root cause.

One example starts with the foreman at a manufacturing plant taking a new trainee manager, who happens to be a systems thinker, on a facility tour. Along the way they see a pool of oil on the floor. The oil is a slipping hazard, and the foreman orders an employee to clean up the spill immediately, but the trainee decides to apply the five whys.

She asks the employee why there was oil on the ground. The answer is that a machine overhead was leaking.

She asks why the machinery was leaking. She learns that the machine was broken.

The foreman is satisfied and tells the employee to fix the machine after he finishes cleaning up the spill, but the trainee presses on: "Why is that machine broken?" The employee replies that the gaskets in the machine were defective.

"And why are the gaskets defective?" she asks. The employee is stumped, except that he had heard that purchasing got a really good deal on them.

By this point, the foreman recognizes that the trainee is on to something. They both dig around a little, make some phone calls, and try to figure out why the company had bought defective gaskets. They discover that the company had adopted a policy of buying the cheapest possible replacement parts without regard to quality or reliability.

Starting with a pool of oil, the two had worked their way back to discover a misguided company policy that had led to the purchase of defective parts. This policy wasn't limited to gaskets: defective replacement parts were causing breakdowns and hazards throughout the plant. The company put a new purchasing policy in effect, and breakdowns became much less frequent.[3]

This is what the "five whys" method of digging down to root causes can do. It can uncover larger issues in a system and suggest fixes that don't just deal with the problem at hand but head off other problems throughout the system.

But as simple as it might be in principle, it can be challenging in practice. Imagine, for instance, that instead of mentioning the defective gaskets, the employee had tried to deflect the blame: "Joe installed that machine. He must have messed it up somehow." Now, instead of following the defective gaskets back to purchasing, our intrepid supervisors would have been questioning Joe's abilities. If you are going to apply the five whys, you want to steer clear of scapegoating. Leave personalities out of it as much as possible.

The five whys can lead us through the levels of thinking. Instead of limiting ourselves to dealing with isolated events, we are more likely to notice patterns. And after seeing the patterns, we can begin to see the flaws in our mental models and gain a better vision of how we can work together:

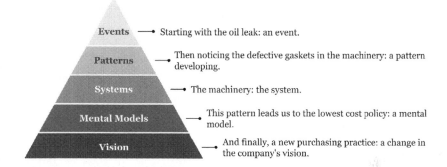

*Graph 02: Iceberg model example*

An individual or a small team can pursue the five whys, but many firms will establish groups to pursue the layers of causality. The team can include anyone affected by the issue and is likely to have insight into action and reaction linkages.

Getting to root causes may take some courage. In 1986, after a devastating disaster at the Chernobyl nuclear power plant in Ukraine, a team of nuclear power experts set out to discover just what led to the explosion that spread radiation across eastern Europe and made several hundred square kilometers of countryside dangerous.

The official story (the first "why" if you will) was that technicians at the plant had botched a reactor safety test. That was true enough; the crew did not run the test properly, and without realizing it, they put the reactor in a very dangerous condition. But that answer didn't fully explain what went wrong. As the test went awry, the crew attempted to shut down the reactor, and that should have prevented the explosion. Something else had gone wrong. The team dug deeper.

What they found was disturbing. Soviet nuclear reactors shared a design flaw: the emergency shutdown process actually caused a brief spike in power before it cut off the reaction. In an emergency, the reactor would get hotter for a few seconds before shutting down and cooling off. Those few seconds of heating were what finally triggered the explosion at the power plant.

And to make matters worse, the Soviet government had known about the flaw, but they treated it as a state secret. Instead of warning plant operators about the problems with the emergency shutdown procedure and correcting the design flaw, the authorities had left power plant staff in the dark and the reactors untouched. And even after the explosion, those same authorities were reluctant to fix the other reactors. The explosion was the consequence of flaws in both the reactor system and the political system.[4]

To be sure, this is an extreme example. It is unlikely you will be dealing with a situation as dire as Chernobyl or policies and practices as maladjusted as those of the Soviet-era nuclear power industry. But the story does illustrate an important point about systems thinking. It can take courage and determination to work through the layers and find root causes. If systems thinking is going to take root in any organization, it helps to have leadership at all levels that are willing to participate and have their own decisions scrutinized.

# 4

# Understanding How Systems Behave

So now we know what systems thinking basically is. We know what a system is, and we have been introduced to one valuable system thinking method: the Five Whys. In a little while, we will show you some more tools that can help you understand how particular systems function, describe your findings to others, and spot problem areas. But first, we will look at how systems function in a more general way.

A healthy system will use **feedback** to sustain itself. Feedback can reinforce and amplify or balance and correct the system's functions.

The passage of **time** can sometimes complicate the operations of a system. The parts of a system do not always respond to each other instantaneously.

Systems have **boundaries**. Systems thinking recognizes that systems can be influenced by environmental conditions outside of the system's influence. The environment is all the things that we must account for, but we cannot adjust ourselves.

There are often **hierarchies** within systems. Sometimes this is explicit, with managers and subordinates. Sometimes this is the practical relationship between systems and subsystems. Understanding the hierarchies will help you to understand how systems respond and what the purposes of all the parts really are.

The various parts of a system will often **synergize**, so the collective result is larger or different from what those same parts would have produced separately.

A system will share and distribute **resources** among its various parts. Observing the stocks and flows – how much is available and how they move – will often be key to understanding a system.

# Feedback: Reinforcing or Balancing?

When they witness some action, most people tend to assume a straight line of cause and effect. Like dominos falling, one thing causes another, which triggers a third thing, then a fourth, and so on. If you go back in time far enough, you will find a first cause that sets the chain in motion; if you go forward far enough, you will see the chain of cause and effect end.

In a system, however, the interconnections between different parts will create loops. Follow effects backward or forward long enough, and some things will begin to repeat, or at least rhyme. Think back to the oxygen cycle: an animal will breathe in oxygen and breathe out carbon dioxide. That carbon dioxide will then be taken in by a tree that will convert it back into oxygen. Then another animal will inhale that oxygen and exhale carbon dioxide. And around it goes.

Two types of cycles are very important. The first is reinforcing cycles. These are cycles that tend to build up and increase in potency or size. Imagine a small room with a sound system: a microphone, a loudspeaker, and an amplifier that is turned up a little bit too high. If someone talks or sings into the mike, the sound from the speaker will reflect off the walls, and some of it will be picked up by the microphone, where it will be amplified and projected out of the speaker, reflect off the walls, re-enter the microphone, and come out of the speaker, this time a little bit louder. Eventually, all the amplified and repeated sounds will create a ringing noise that can drown out all the other sounds in the room. Sound technicians call this ringing "feedback." Systems thinkers would call this feedback too: reinforcing feedback, to be precise. Reinforcing feedback can overwhelm a system, defeating its purpose.[5]

Reinforcing cycles can also be good. Imagine an investment account. The account is managed well, and it is earning money. If enough of the earnings are reinvested, the potential earnings will escalate. The cycle of earning and reinvestment will create more and more money for the investors.

Feedback can also lead to balance, or at least a bit of back and forth around an average that the system can handle reasonably well. Imagine we're back in the room. (We've turned the amplifier down, so that awful ringing is gone.) There is a thermostat on the wall, so when it gets too hot, the air conditioner comes on and cools it. And when the room gets too cool, the furnace turns on to warm it. The room now has balanced feedback, as the thermostat governs the temperature.

There will still be cycles. In the summer, the heat outside and the sun coming through the windows will warm the room up until the heat trips the thermostat, which turns the A/C on. Now the room cools down until the thermostat trips again, turning the A/C off, at which point the room starts warming up again. But whether the air conditioning is on or off, the room should be reasonably comfortable all day long.

At Isle Royale National Park in Michigan, biologists noticed a fascinating pattern with the wildlife. Over time wolf packs and moose herds have migrated to the island, crossing Lake Superior when ice forms in the winter. The wolves hunted the moose, sometimes to the brink of elimination. But when the moose herds were at their lowest, the wolf population would shrink as prey became harder to find. With fewer threats from the wolves, the moose population would recover. The system sometimes shifted dramatically over time, but while the populations went up and down, the relationship between predators and prey provided checks on their numbers, until recently when a decline in wolves led to excessive inbreeding.[6]

## Time: Delayed Reactions

To understand how systems function, it is important to pay attention to timing. The parts of a system may be closely related to one another, but they do not always act simultaneously. It may take anywhere from minutes to years (especially for geological or natural systems) for one part of a system to respond to activity in another part.

This delay can complicate attempts to understand a system's inner workings. Biology will compensate for a forest fire: animal and plant life will move into the burned-out area, but the effect may take years to become apparent to the untrained eye.

Sometimes delays result in a system breakdown. Imagine a recently opened gym. The gym is in a prime location, and it has the most up-to-date equipment: treadmills, exercise bikes, weightlifting equipment, and everything else. The gym's owners are aggressively recruiting new members, and word of mouth means their membership drive is successful.

Too successful, it turns out. As new members join, the chances that they will find a vacant bike or weightlifting bench start to drop. Existing equipment is overused, and maintenance slips. That means even less equipment is available, which adds to the frustration. But the gym's owners don't realize what's going on. Membership is peaking, so the gym is making plenty of money. New members keep signing up until the word gets out: this gym is overcrowded, and the equipment is in poor shape. New memberships dry up, and existing members cancel or let their memberships expire.

Now, weeks or months after customers started noticing the problem, management sees memberships and revenue dropping, and they are finally aware that they need to pay closer attention to the gym's capacity and equipment maintenance.

Without that delay, the gym's owners might have scaled back their membership drive in time to prevent overcrowding and put more resources into equipment maintenance. Those actions would have kept their customers satisfied. Then they might have looked into the possibility of expanding their location or adding a new gym nearby, so they could serve the larger market.

A good systems thinker will look for delays and try to minimize them or even try to anticipate changes and turn them into opportunities. For instance, the gym's owners might survey their members periodically or encourage staff at the gym to pass along positive or negative feedback that they get from customers. The more complete and up-to-date the information available within the system, the better it will function.[7]

## Boundaries: The System and Its Environment

One of the trickier aspects of systems thinking is the question of boundaries. What is in the system, and what is outside of it? As a basic rule, the system includes all the entities that are necessary for the system to function and are controlled by the system's management.

You will often find that there are factors that are outside of your influence that can affect your system and that you need to account for. For instance, think of the room with its furnace and air conditioning. The weather will certainly affect conditions in the room. The furnace will be working a lot more in the winter, while the A/C will be on a lot more during the summer. But the seasons will change no matter what temperature the thermostat is set at. These outside factors that can affect a system are referred to as the environment. For systems thinking, the environment isn't limited to nature. For instance, if there is a power outage during the summer, the air conditioning won't work at all. The risk of an outage would also be considered part of the environment for system thinking purposes.

What is in or out of a system can be the subject of debate. For instance, imagine a college that offers online courses. The online course program is a system with students receiving instruction from professors, asking questions, and then doing coursework that the professors evaluate. There will typically be a final exam or project at the end of the year, and students will receive their grades. All the information is passed back and forth through the internet.

Is the internet itself part of the system? Certainly, it is a key component; the online education system cannot function without it. And the college probably has an IT department to work on any technical problems that might come up, giving them at least some influence over the web's operations. But the web is incredibly large, and the college's influence on it is quite modest. The best approach will be for the college to treat the internet as part of its environment, something they will need to account for but is largely outside of their control.[8]

As you think about the systems that you deal with, you will have to set boundaries and accept that some things are outside of your reach, even if there is some chance they will affect your system or be influenced by it in some way. Otherwise, you will find yourself contemplating the sky, the sun, moon, and stars, the whole cosmos. Systems thinking should ultimately be practical. Your focus should be the things that you or your team has some meaningful influence over, and your environmental factors should mainly be forces that you can account for or the risks you can foresee.

# Hierarchies: Who's in Charge and Why Are We Doing This?

System thinkers recognize two types of hierarchies. The first is the one you're probably most familiar with, the "chain of command." This is the power relationship between people working in a system. The general manager directs the assistant managers, who in turn direct the rest of the employees. There may also be informal relationships that can turn the formal organizational chart around a bit: one of the employees may have more seniority and experience than the others, so the rest of the team defers to her or him even though they all have the same job title. If that employee has enough experience, some of the junior managers may rely on them for input or ask them to train new staff members. But whether there's a formal organizational chart or informal relationships that determine assignments and accountability, there is bound to be some sort of hierarchy among people working in any system.

The second sort of hierarchy is between a large system and the subsystems within it. For instance, imagine a bakery that ships bread to supermarkets throughout its hometown. That bakery is a system that takes raw ingredients, mixes them into a dough, bakes the loaves, packages them, and then ships them out to the markets. The shipping operation will be a system of its own: a subsystem composed of trucks, drivers, and loading equipment.

These two types of hierarchies may seem very different. One is composed entirely of people and organized according to who supervises whom; the second is made up of larger and smaller systems. But a very similar principle applies to both: just as the superior authority in a human hierarchy directs the people below her in a human hierarchy, the operations of a subsystem, the work it performs, the resources available to it, even the challenges it must overcome, will be determined by the place it holds in the larger system.[9] The shipping department exists to deliver bread produced by the bakery. The trucks will be modified to deliver bread. It will have enough trucks to cover its regular delivery schedule, but probably not many more than that. The drivers' routes will be set up to cover the bakery's customers. And if there is a delay in producing bread, the shipping department will need to adjust, maybe by waiting to send one of its trucks out on its route or by sending out an additional truck, later on, to make up shortages.

Again, it is important to set boundaries when you look at hierarchies. As Australian professor of Media Studies J.T. Velikovsky has observed, all of reality can arguably be described by nested levels of systems, starting from particles that form atoms to chemicals that support life to social systems and governments, and on to our planet, the solar system, the galaxy, and the universe.[10]

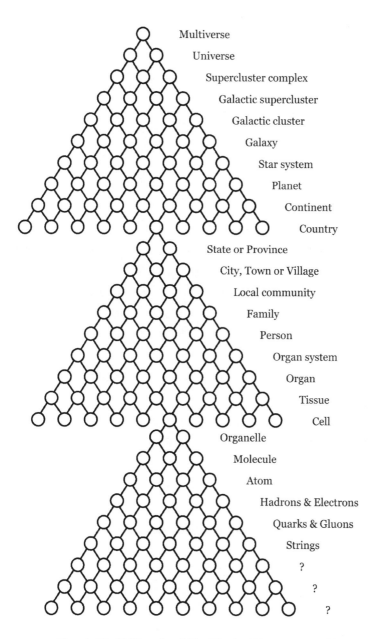

Multiverse
Universe
Supercluster complex
Galactic supercluster
Galactic cluster
Galaxy
Star system
Planet
Continent
Country
State or Province
City, Town or Village
Local community
Family
Person
Organ system
Organ
Tissue
Cell
Organelle
Molecule
Atom
Hadrons & Electrons
Quarks & Gluons
Strings
?
?
?

*Graph 03: Velikovsky, J.T. - Vertical Integration of Systems*

This grand hierarchy can be useful for understanding systems, as long as you don't take it too far. The purpose of systems thinking is to help us to understand and improve the systems we work with, not to have us contemplating ever-larger systems "to infinity and beyond!"

# Synergy: "Teamwork Makes the Dream Work"

Synergy is one of those words that sounds sophisticated and maybe a bit mysterious, but the basic idea is fairly straightforward: in a team or a system that works well together, the whole is greater than the sum of its parts. "Synergy" is the way that the parts work together to produce a desirable result. Synergy can happen in a collection of people: a basketball team that plays well together. The players anticipating each other's movements as they pass and dribble or play defense display synergy that creates open shots and denies their opponents scoring chances. Synergy can arise in arts and entertainment, as a band or a comedy troupe pools its talents.

Likewise, the parts in a well-designed device can display synergy. A modern cellular phone is very synergistic, using the cellular phone data stream to provide access to email, webpages, messages, maps, and games, all through one small screen. Modern smartphones have basically the same parts - processor, battery, screen, camera, etc. How much utility users get from a smartphone highly depends on how well these parts work together - display synergies. Technology companies such as Apple, Google, and Samsung compete on building and fine-tuning different operating systems (iOS, Android, etc.) to maximize synergies and improve performance.

How exactly synergy comes about will vary from system to system. On a basketball team, the synergy will be the players' complementary skills and the precision and timing of their movement that puts opponents at a disadvantage. For a musical combo, synergy will be the pooling of creative ideas that produces rich, multilayered music. In a machine, synergy may consist of a design that makes the best use of technology, space, and materials, so the parts fit and move together precisely, resulting in an excellent performance.

In short, synergy is a lot like teamwork, except it applies to both people and things in a system.

## Stocks and Flows

Systems store, move around, use, and produce resources. Those resources might be raw materials, money, energy, or ideas. Wherever a resource builds up – wood in a woodpile, parts in a warehouse, or money in an account – they are called "stocks." When they shift – wood is fed into a fire, or a part is taken off a shelf and installed, or an invoice is paid off – that is called a flow.

You can track these stocks and flows as they work their way through a system. Imagine a river is dammed in several places. A lake forms behind one of these dams, and that lake is used for fishing and recreation. There are homes, a marina, maybe a small town on the shores of the lake. That lake, along with the dam, is a system, and the water is a resource. The water in the lake right now will be a stock, and the dams' operators will want to keep a close eye on that stock. If it gets too low, the boaters won't be able to take their boats out of the marina. If it goes too high, the nearby homes and the town will be flooded.

Water will flow into and out of the lake. Some flows cannot be controlled: water will evaporate from the surface, and rain will fall in. Fortunately, some flows can be controlled: the dam's gates can be opened or closed, and there is another dam further up the river that could also be opened up if there is a drought and water levels drop too far. These are the things to look for when you are examining a system.

Next, we will show you some graphic tools that can help you to visualize a system's inner workings and explain them to others.

# 5

# Mapping Systems

We've talked about all the things that go into a system and how they interact with each other to create feedback and synergy. Now let's look at some graphics that system thinkers have developed to help them create a mental picture of a system and explain it to others.

The first step to understanding a system is determining just what its parts are and mapping out how all the parts relate to one another. One way to do this is to create a connection diagram. You can do this by yourself, or you can make this a brainstorming exercise for a group, in which you take suggestions about all the things that you might include in your system. Once you've looked at these, you can start to settle on your system's boundaries, discarding the items that aren't relevant. You might decide to combine some items, treating them as subsystems. Then you can determine which parts influence others.

For instance, the connection chart for the room with the thermostat might look like this:

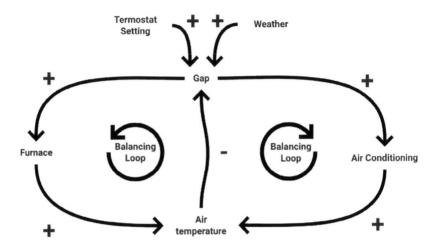

*Graph 04: Connection chart thermostat*

This chart shows that the thermostat controls the furnace and the air conditioning. The thermostat's actions are affected by the temperature of the air in the room. The air temperature is influenced by the furnace, the A/C, and also by the weather outside. There is nothing in the system that will affect the weather; that is part of the system's environment.

You can also see the matching feedback loops: If you follow the arrows, you can see how room temperature affects the thermostat, which turns on either the furnace or the A/C, and these either raise or lower the air temperature, completing the loop.

Suppose you want to watch one variable to see how the system performs. Is the air conditioning working well on a hot day? This is what we call "behavior over time." Here's how that might look:

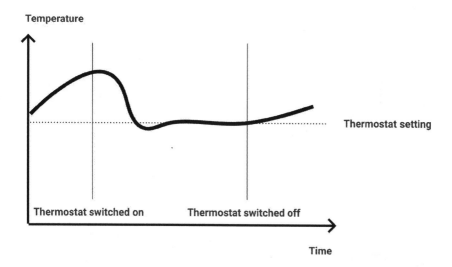

*Graph 05: Temperature over time in summer (balancing feedback)*

That looks all right. You can see the changes when the thermostat turned the air conditioning on and off. This is what balancing feedback will do. The system acts to counteract changes. There is some back and forth, but the temperature stays within a fairly narrow range.

What happened when the amplifier on the sound system was turned up too high?

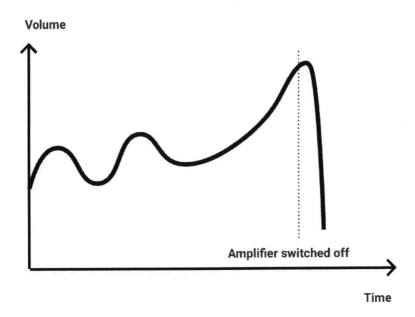

*Graph 06: Volume over time (reinforcing feedback)*

The volume in the room is okay for a while, but as the feedback builds up, it accelerates until it becomes unbearable. This is what happens when a reinforcing feedback loop runs out of control.

Suppose you want to illustrate the stocks and flows of a resource within a system. Here is what the stock and flow map would look like for the water in the lake behind the dam:

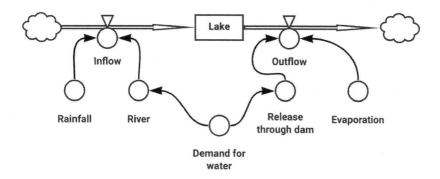

*Graph 07: Stock and flow lake behind the dam*

These take a little more explaining. As a general rule, in stock and flow diagrams, stocks are represented by squares or rectangles. In this case, the big rectangle in the center is the stock of water in the lake. The clouds on either end represent "sources" or "sinks," basically all the water that our model does not account for, going into and out of our system.

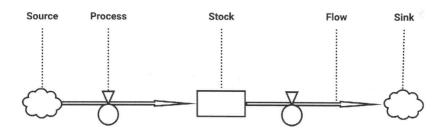

*Graph 08: Stock and flow diagrams explained*

Including sources and sinks means that we are admitting that this model does not include all the factors that might affect the water level. This is an "open system." A "closed system" is one that is not or cannot be affected by anything outside of the model. A closed system will begin and end with stocks.

The double lines represent the flows, and the circles that are connected to those double lines show where the flows come from and go to. Here we have water flowing into the river and rainfall flowing into the lake, and we have water flowing out via evaporation and releases through the dam.

There is an additional factor here: a circle that is set off from the flow, representing the demand for water in the region. That circle is what is called a converter. This converter is connected to two other circles (one of them represents water flowing into the river, the other represents water released from the dam) by single lines. These single lines represent information. There is no water going directly along these lines (so you should never see an information line connecting directly to a stock), but demand for water in the area surrounding the lake, for drinking, bathing, cleaning, and local industries, will affect how much water flows into the lake. If there is more demand for water, more water will be drawn from the river before it gets to the lake, and the operator of the dam will find himself under public pressure to release more water to communities further down the river.

Using a stock and flow graphic, you can see how things like weather and public water use will affect the flow of water into the lake and the overall level of water in the lake. You may also see a graphic that shows the stocks and flows of more than one resource and uses information lines and converters to show things that can influence both resources. For instance, we might add a stock and flow diagram for electricity generated at the dam and show how an increase in population in the area would increase the demand for both. Then we could show the relationships between the water and electrical systems. That could become a complicated chart, but it could be very useful to local utility planners as they prepare for a growing population.

Causal loop graphics show us the steps that a system goes through and illustrates how feedback can make a system work or break down. Let's start with one of the simplest, the reinforcing feedback loop.

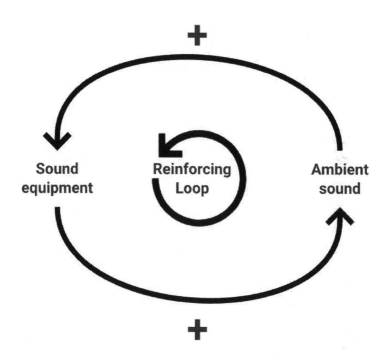

*Graph 09: Reinforcing feedback loop sound system*

As you can see, it's a circle made up of two arrows and two stages. On the right, you have the ambient sound in the room, and on the left, you have the sound equipment, the microphone, amplifier, and speaker, which pick up the ambient sound and reproduce it, only louder. This increases the volume of the sound in the room, which reverberates back to the microphone.

Now, let's go back to the air conditioning example. Here we account for the thermostat, which keeps things in check.

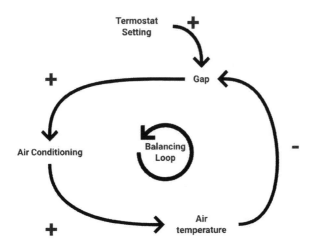

*Graph 10: Connection chart thermostat single loop*

As long as the temperature is not too high, there is no action taken in this loop. The thermostat setting is made outside of the causal loop; that means whoever controls the thermostat can set it wherever he or she likes, and the room temperature will adjust and hold steady at that level.

We can add a second loop to account for the heating system and show that the system will balance year-round.

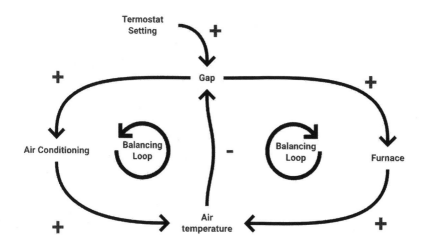

*Graph 11: Connection chart thermostat double loop*

These feedback graphics can show you the stages of a cycle, a cycle that you might want to reinforce, control, or prevent. By going through the stages, you can identify interventions that will stop cycles from getting out of hand.

Let's go back to our sound equipment. We don't want to get rid of it because someone is going to give a speech in a little while, and there will be a lot of people coming to hear it. But we can add a volume control.

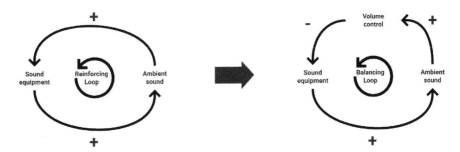

*Graph 12: Balancing feedback loop sound system with volume control*

The volume control adjusts the amplifier, reducing sound output when needed to prevent feedback. The controller adds a new variable to the original loop, showing its relationship to the amplifier. Now the sound equipment should work fine, and everyone will be able to hear the speech without the annoying ringing noise.

Drawing up these charts will help you to get a handle on all aspects of a system. Connection graphics help you determine the parts of a system, the relationships between the parts, and the boundaries between the system and its environment. Behavior over time charts help you see how systems change and how they adjust to maintain balance. Stocks and Flows charts show where resources are located and how they move through a system. Finally, causal loop diagrams show the repeating stages that create feedback. A good systems thinker will be familiar with all of these graphics and will know how to use them to illustrate the inner workings of systems, spot potential problems, and find solutions.[11]

# 6

# Common Patterns and How to Deal With Them

There are many ways that a system can go off the rails. This chapter will discuss some of the more common ones. We will also show you feedback loop graphics that illustrate these problems and suggest ways to counteract them.[12]

## Drifting Goals: Accepting Mediocre

Most of us have made New Year's Resolutions to exercise more or spend less money or eat less junk food or learn a new skill. And we have all learned how hard it can be to make positive changes or reach for new goals; even when we succeed, it is likely to be only after stumbles and multiple attempts. The temptation to settle for a little less is part of human nature. It can also be a system problem.

From a systems standpoint, the problem of drifting goals begins with a persistent gap between results and objectives: a "performance gap." Once someone in an organization sees the gap, there are two ways that the organization can respond: it can take corrective action to bring performance up to standards, or it can accept the result. Over time, accepting the current result means adopting that as the new standard.

The parody motivational poster says: "Hard work often pays off over time, but laziness always pays off now."[13] Unfortunately, there's a lot of truth to that: taking corrective action involves extra effort, and success is not guaranteed. In addition, even if the corrections are effective, there is likely to be some delay before improvements show up. And other pressures might push an organization toward accepting lowered standards. High production quotas or a tight delivery schedule might push leadership to look the other way at quality or safety issues.

But once that shortcut is taken, it becomes easier to continue to go down the same path, creating a feedback loop that turns a moment of laxity or a temporary expedient into an established practice. The causal loops will look something like this:

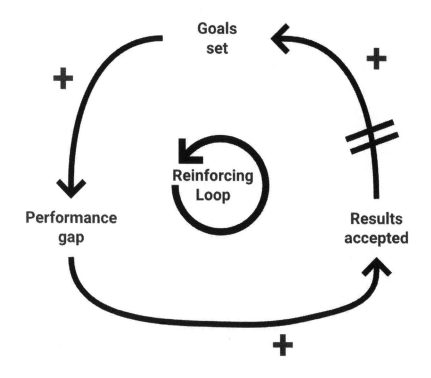

*Graph 13: Drifting Goals*

This is sometimes referred to as the "boiled frog syndrome." A frog will jump away quickly after a sharp temperature increase but will sit still while heat increases gradually, even up to the point where it is fatal. Likewise an organization will react to a sudden drop in performance but might tolerate a gradual decline until there is a crisis. If you see a gradual decline in performance, there is a good chance you are dealing with a drifting goals situation.

Responding to drifting goals should start by looking at the process and the incentives that lead to goal setting. Ideally, standards should be set by a rational process, preferably one that uses some outside standard. An institution-wide commitment to constant improvement can be useful. So can regular investigation and reference to customer expectations or standards set by competitors that your organization should be ready to meet or exceed. These external standards can be a check on the temptation to settle for less. As you can see in the graph, the feedback loop is still reinforcing, however, in a positive direction, driving continuous improvement and innovation.

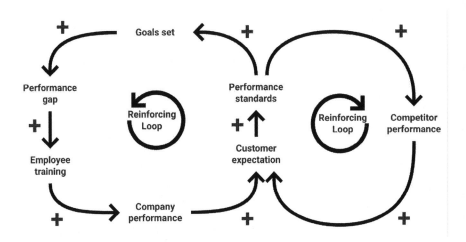

*Graph 14: Goals based on external standards*

Goals and standards should be set transparently and widely distributed. If you want the divisions in your organization to stretch themselves, you should reward your teams for setting aggressive goals and avoid imposing any penalties for failing to meet them immediately.

# Escalation: Mutual Threats

When two adversaries square off, there is a risk that hostilities will spiral out of control. That process of provocation and response can become a cycle of escalation that can harm all involved even if they manage to avoid the absolute worst outcome.

Systems thinking sees escalation as a feedback loops that can become reinforcing:

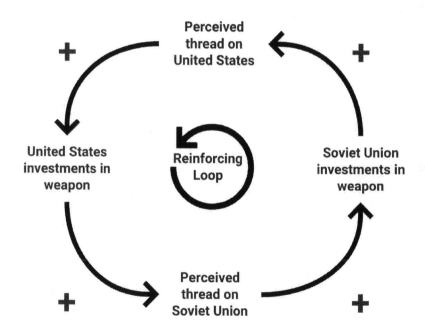

*Graph 15: Cycle of escalation in the Cold War*

The classic escalation scenario was the "cold war" between the United States and the Soviet Union. The two nations eyed each other warily, with each nation developing and testing new weapons and maneuvering diplomatically. Every technical or diplomatic advance by one nation was likely to be perceived as damaging to national prestige, influence, or security by the other. This would provoke a response, which in turn would be taken as a threat.

But international geopolitics isn't the only realm where one might see escalation cycles. Any field where there are two powerful, more-or-less evenly matched competitors in a zero-sum competition can devolve into a cycle of escalation. Two companies with similar products and prices competing for the same market can find themselves in a cycle of escalating price cuts that damage both firms.

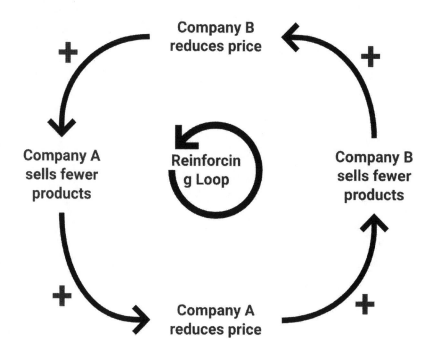

*Graph 16: Cycle of escalation in product pricing*

As one company reduces prices, the other sees itself losing customers and responds by reducing its price even further to make up for a lost market share. And the first company responds further. The cycle might benefit customers, at least in the short run, but both companies find themselves with diminished profits or even taking losses, leaving them without funds for customer service, marketing, or research and development. Eventually, even consumers may be harmed as the companies exhaust themselves.

In the early 1980s, Texas Instruments found itself confronting Commodore in what was then a modest-but-growing personal computer market. The TI-99/4a was close in performance to Commodore's VIC-20. The two responded to each other with a series of price reductions that made their products unprofitable. The TI-99/4a debuted with a $525 price tag, but in the end, it could be had for under $100. The conflict didn't just affect prices. Texas Instruments, which always had a policy of discouraging third-party software development, had no flexibility to change because selling software and peripherals was their best chance to recoup losses. Commodore, for its part, developed a reputation for treating its dealers poorly.

Whether it's about price tags or missiles, the way out of this cycle of confrontation and retaliation begins with at least one party questioning basic assumptions. Parties can begin by asking whether this competition is necessary. Who is their rival? And what is the key field of competition? Is it price or military strength or something else entirely? The parties should also examine their assumptions about the other party's intentions. Look for delays and other aspects that might lead one party or the other to have a distorted view of the threats facing them. An act that is perceived as hostile may only be defensive in nature; it may not be necessary to respond in kind to every action taken by the other side.

All of this leads to the essential concluding question: can one party or the other shift their strategy to lessen the conflict? For instance, either Texas Instruments or Commodore might have done better by modifying their systems to compete on performance rather than price.

In a cycle of escalation, one might hope to outlast the adversary, but those hopes are often misplaced. Commodore would declare bankruptcy, while Texas Instruments would sell off its personal computer line. In a zero-sum game, one would assume there will be a winner, but that distinction could just as easily go to a third party, such as Apple or Microsoft. One is almost always better off finding a creative way out of the single-minded conflict.

# Fixes That Fail: Here We Go Again...

Sometimes the cure can be worse than the disease. In a "fixes that fail," scenario the cure can even become part of the disease. A temporary measure intended to alleviate a problem can provide temporary relief. And if all you have is a temporary problem, that might be enough. But what if there is an underlying problem that isn't being addressed?

Imagine our bakery has picked up a big new customer but hasn't realized that they need to add capacity: more ovens or more trucks to make deliveries. For a while, they muddle through with bakery staff and truck drivers logging overtime. But deliveries start to fall behind. Now one of their customers calls to ask where their shipment is. The managers rush to get that customer's order out the door. But all the other orders get delayed. Or quality suffers when mixing and baking operations get thrown out-of-whack. ("...usually it takes an hour to bake our hamburger buns, but we'll pull these out ten minutes early so we can get them on the truck in time...") Now there are more frustrated customers and more phone calls.

Or go back to the sore knee hypothetical. There are times when taking the pain medication works just fine. But what if there's something seriously wrong with the knee, like a damaged tendon? Your decision to treat the pain and go on with all your regular activities like your daily jog will only aggravate the injury. The pain will come back and probably get worse.

Over time your pain level might look something like this:

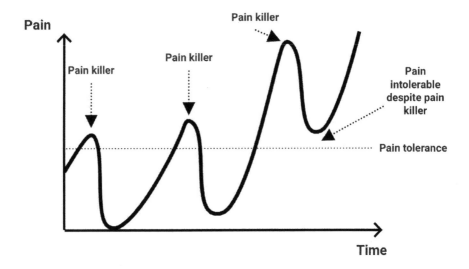

*Graph 17: Pain vs. time*

Eventually, even a full dose of painkillers won't completely alleviate the symptoms.

There are many ways for a fix to fail, but they all have two things in common: there is an underlying issue that goes unaddressed, so the fix has unintended consequences, and the symptom comes back.

For the bakery, the unintended consequence is the disruption to their operations as they rush orders out. For your knee, it might be the stress you put on it while the painkillers last.

Dealing with a "fixes that fail" scenario begins with recognizing the pattern and committing to finding a permanent solution for the bakery that will likely mean adding capacity. For the man or woman suffering from a sore knee, the first step is probably to schedule a visit to a doctor and follow the course of treatment. Dealing with the underlying issue may mean continuing with the temporary fix while a permanent solution is implemented. The bakery staff may wind up working a lot of overtime until the new oven is installed. Your doctor may recommend you take it easy on your knee and give it a chance to heal properly on its own, or she might schedule surgery. But either way, you'll probably need to continue taking pain medication for a while; your doctor might even prescribe something stronger.

But this is why it is so important to look for patterns, think about larger systems, and be ready to question your assumptions. The sooner you start, the sooner you can find and deal with the real issue, and the less damage you or your organization will suffer. We all deal with fixes that fail from time to time. The first step back is simply to recognize that your short-term fix is a long-term failure. Once you have recognized that, you can diagnose the longer-term problem and begin to deal with it.

# Success to the Successful: The Rich Get Richer, up to a Point

In any industry where competitiveness is valued, there is a risk that one team will gain an advantage. As rewards and resources continue to flow to that one team, its challengers will be starved for the material and talent they need to compete. This can be a great situation if you happen to be a member of that singular winning team, at least for a little while. But what if that competition becomes so lopsided that it undermines the long-term health of the larger system?

The "Success to the Successful scenario" can take many forms. In a company, there might be the sales team that gets the more lucrative leads on account of past results. In a family, you might have a sibling who gets more emotional support and encouragement because he or she is perceived to be more responsible than the others. This creates a pair of reinforcing feedback loops, where one person or team continues to receive more support, is able to generate better results, and consequently continues to receive additional support.

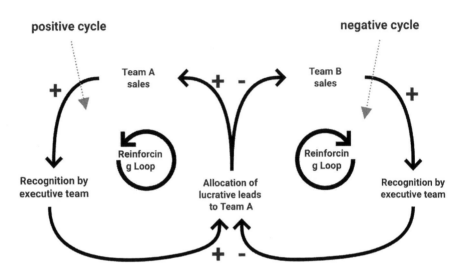

*Graph 18: "Success to the Successful" - competing sales teams*

You don't even need separate entities competing with one another; the competition might be entirely inside the head of one person who has to balance two roles. A busy executive might feel driven to spend more and more time at the office, where his extra effort is appreciated, as opposed to his home, which is becoming more and more stressful. As he puts more and more of his time at the office, the contrast only grows sharper.

In the short term, this course of action might make some sense: whether it's teams in a business or children in a family, you want to establish incentives to reward good performance and discourage poor performance. It is only human nature to put our energy into the activities we enjoy, and good sense to concentrate on the areas where we excel.

But the incentives we create and the choices we make about our personal time and effort have to be made with the larger system in mind. Not everything is meant to be a winner-take-all competition.

How to deal with a "success to the successful" scenario depends on how one wants the system to evolve. The first question to be considered is whether or not the internal competition should continue. Or to look at it another way: would the purposes of this system be better served by creating a more harmonious relationship between the various parts? Should there even be a separation?

Our executive would almost certainly benefit from thinking about home and office less as competing claims on his time and more as complementary parts of a whole and satisfying life. Doing so would mean recognizing that a stressful family life is dragging down his own system of relationships and that he should put more of his time and energy into restoring those relationships.

The business with its two competing sales teams might achieve greater synergy by combining the two squads into a single sales team. At the very least, there is an opportunity for new collaborations between former rivals that could prove very fruitful. The incentives that might have been created by competition between two teams could be stimulated by setting ambitious goals and challenging them to stay on a path of continuous improvement, encouraging them to compete against themselves.

If you want to maintain a competitive dynamic, you should recognize that interventions will be needed to maintain a level playing field. The best example of this might be professional sports in North America. All four of the major North American sports leagues: the NFL, NBA, NHL, and Major League Baseball, have established player drafts that give the weaker teams the first chance to claim the best young talent.

This process counteracts the tendency for the best players to gravitate to the wealthiest and most successful teams. Given enough time, this can turn the reinforcing feedback that keeps traditional powers on top into balancing feedback that allows weaker teams to rise. (It especially helps if one of the struggling teams brings in new management with a sharp eye for new talent.) The draft doesn't level everything all at once. Great teams, even dynasties, have emerged over time. But the equalizing factor of the player draft means that struggling teams and their fans can say "just wait 'til next year" with a reasonable hope that next year will be different. That competitive dynamic makes for a more interesting and exciting game.

These are just a few of the common scenarios that arise in systems thinking, along with some common observations about how they arise and how they can be corrected. The key to recognizing and addressing all of these is seeing the entire system and how feedback in a system can create causal loops that aggravate problems. Once you see the feedback, you can counteract it or create a different system that avoids the feedback entirely.

# 7

# Applying Systems Thinking

With the toolkit of system thinking, there are many levels one can address a problem at. Going back to our iceberg model:

- You can react to events.
- You can adapt to patterns.
- You can improve the current or create a new system.
- You can question and adjust your mental model.
- You can generate a new vision.

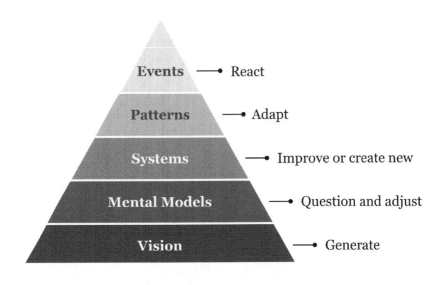

*Graph 19: How to address a problem*

Which one is best is for you to determine.[14] Sometimes an event is just that: a one-time incident that doesn't require top-to-bottom changes. But the ability to look at the larger system and create new systems that are better at fulfilling their purposes can be empowering and life-changing.

This chapter will look at several areas, including a few controversial social issues, where systems thinking might be applied. Because this is an introductory book, we will keep our discussion at a high level. These examples are meant to be suggestive and open up different ways of thinking, not to be the last word.

Using the tools of systems thinking, you are more likely to see the larger pattern, less likely to be thrown off by the details of a particular incident. For instance, suppose your spouse objects to your taking part in some activity, such as visiting a friend or pursuing a hobby. Now maybe they object to your friend or your recreational choices, but if you can think of your relationship with your spouse as a system, you can put this particular argument in a larger context. You can look for other causes of disagreement and possibly spot a different causal loop.

Maybe this isn't about your friend. Maybe your spouse just wants to spend more time with you. That's certainly something that she might want. As you consider that possibility, you might recall another afternoon when the same friend visited, and the three of you spent a pleasant afternoon talking about favorite movies. No, you realize, this isn't about my friendships. It's about time. And you can respond accordingly.

System thinking certainly is valuable in business; it is frequently taught to managers at all levels of many different types of companies. Going back to our example of the gym that lost customers because it didn't have the equipment available to serve its members, system thinking could have helped the gym avoid that worst-case scenario. By thinking of their facility as a system, they would have seen the problem sooner or maybe anticipated it and avoided it entirely. They could have worked for a balance that would keep their membership at a level where all were satisfied or looked for opportunities to invest and expand.

System thinking has been critical to the rise of Toyota Motor Corporation, and Toyota was an early testing ground for many system thinking ideas. The company's founder, Senkichi Toyoda, is credited as the creator of the "five whys" method of problem-solving. Its corporate philosophy, the "Toyota Way," and its approach to manufacturing, the "Toyota Production System" are both laced with systems thinking. The company's approach encourages managers to stop production if needed to fix problems. The decision-making process is intentionally deliberate and consensus-based in order to allow for all those affected to speak and all impacts to be considered. The company is committed to constant learning and continuous improvement.[15] These practices have made Toyota one of the world's largest automakers, allowing it to expand its operations far from its Japanese homeland. The company has even found success in the United States, right under the noses of the powerful "Big Three."

Toyota's experience points to another important aspect of systems thinking: to make the best use of this toolkit in an organization, it should not just be an incidental thing, a technique that the organization uses once every few years to deal with a single knotty problem. Ideally, it should be adopted as part of the system itself. As system thinking is used, the organization will build up knowledge of its own systems. This is how the "learning organization" that Toyota has built itself into works. That institutional knowledge gives Toyota a head start on every issue it contends with; they know their own systems well.

A company may go back to the systems thinking toolbox several times as it implements change. For instance, when Sabre Holdings, the Texas-based company that operates Travelocity and other online travel services, decided to reduce the waste it sent to the landfill by 80 percent, they repeatedly went back to systems thinking as they worked out the hows and whys of its commitment to go green.

Starting with a close examination of its own trash, the company examined its stocks and flows of waste and confirmed that less than 20 percent of its waste needed to go to the dump. The rest could be recycled or composted. As the company made and implemented its plan, attention was paid to the shape and location of waste receptacles, as Sabre's "Eco Team" learned that proper disposal of waste depended on them being convenient and designed to handle the waste. The bins for compostable waste had to be redesigned with a wider opening to handle the "clamshell" boxes used at the company cafeteria.

As Sabre worked on reducing landfill waste, the company made more adjustments to the waste handling system. Employees were encouraged to bring their own drinking glasses and coffee mugs, reducing the number of disposable cups that went into waste. Sabre added a training program to the new employee orientation process to ensure that all staff understood the system and were ready to do their part to minimize waste.

Sabre Holdings eventually achieved its goals, but they didn't achieve this green result with a single ingenious fix. They did it by developing their understanding of how waste was created on-site and how their own system for disposing of waste operated. With that knowledge, they implemented and then adjusted their plan, achieving and cementing their goals.[16]

## Systems Thinking and Education

Systems thinking could be used to solve many societal problems. For instance, public education is subpar in many American communities. Too many children are not learning even the basics of reading, writing, science, and math, let alone being prepared to work or contribute to the larger society. Public schools are a political logjam, with numerous constituencies at cross purposes. Applying systems thinking could cut through all of the agendas, encouraging parents, teachers, and staff to reach a consensus about the purposes schools serve and refocus the debate on how to achieve those ends. With its rigid progression through standardized grades, curricula, and evaluations, the current model of education might give way to something more flexible and adaptable to the strengths of students. The school year may change from one that is punctuated by long summer breaks to a year-round model with shorter school days but fewer long interruptions. Instead of moving in a single cohort, we might see students progressing at their own pace, advancing when they are ready to move to the next level or branching off into a specialty that fits their unique abilities.

We might reimagine the classroom, allowing classes to cross-subject matter boundaries. One class might stage a mock trial to learn about the justice system, but in the process, choose a case that involves a strong scientific component, allowing students to learn about both government and the scientific method. Systems thinking might also lead to more opportunities for parents to choose schools and teachers that best fit their children's needs.

This process of reinventing our education system and reorienting it towards its central role in society is our best chance of cutting through the political gridlock.[17]

## Systems Thinking and Social Media

Among the many pressing problems facing society today is the role of social media. The internet has served extremely well as a means of communication through electronic mail, websites, and data transfers. The creation of social media systems such as Facebook and Twitter were initially hailed as the latest advances in communication, providing creative new ways for people to share news and interests. Social media has turned sour in the eyes of many, faulted for spreading rumors, innuendo, and conspiracy theories, for violating users' privacy, aggravating social divisions and unrest, and generally being damaging to mental well-being. And all this has taken place at a time when social media has replaced traditional media as the main source of news.

The Artefact Group, a Seattle-based design and consulting firm, investigated and issued its own systems thinking-based report on social media and found several causal loops in social media. These causal loops arise naturally out of the worldwide-web architecture and capabilities, the incentives of social media companies, and users' experiences and interests. These causal loops all tend to create social media that are sensationalistic, individually tailored, and alienating.[18]

The primary interest of social media companies is to maximize the attention they get from users; get as many of them as you can and keep them staring at your screens as long as possible. Social media companies do this by creating streams of data that cater to individual interests. This information works best for media companies when it is as engaging as possible. Unfortunately, the computerized systems that assemble and present this data cannot sift accurate news or informed opinion from wildly speculative or even patently false material. The result is a race to the bottom on several levels.

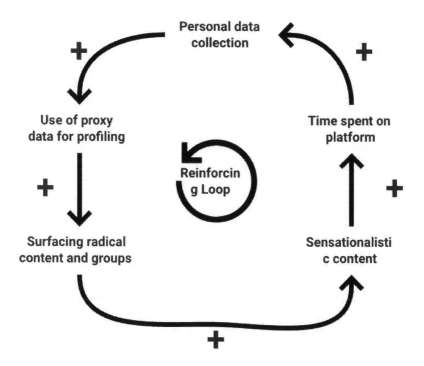

*Graph 20: Social Media race to bottom*[19]

While this is going on, the social media company's most devoted users spend more and more time online, in cyberspace instead of "physical space," where humans contact each other in person. Humans can adapt to electronic communications, but they evolved to communicate and relate to others by direct sight, sound, and touch. Social media can disrupt the real-world communication people need to thrive, and this can produce anxiety and depression, making the most devoted users more sympathetic to sensationalist, extreme, and ultimately radicalizing content.

Artefact has identified three interventions that might break the negative feedback loops of social media systems.

- Regulation protecting privacy: social media companies can mine a great deal of private information about their users, which they use to micro-target the data that users see. This microtargeting allows social media to find specific messages that will get users' immediate attention and keep them plugged in. By limiting the companies' access to user information, this targeting will be much less precise. The user experience might be less immediately engaging in the short term, but users will be more likely to find articles and links that are outside of their typical preferences. This broadening of sources will diminish the extent to which social media cement users' opinions and preferences, leading to less radicalization. The report recommends that data privacy be treated as a fundamental right and suggests that lawmakers use the European Union's General Data Protection Regulation as a starting point.

- Develop new measures for success: Currently, social media companies measure success almost entirely in terms of user time spent engaging with their own social media system. They then sell users' attention to advertisers. This advertiser-centered economic model may be about to hit its peak economic value. The report suggests that social media firms look for new economic models, developing metrics that account for quality as well as quantity of engagement, and develop revenue streams outside of advertising.

- Finally, social media should look to improve the user experience holistically. This means developing algorithms for presenting material to users that bridge divisions and creates common ground rather than polarizing and driving people apart. Social media should also find ways to encourage healthy relationships between users, perhaps by presenting ways for users to connect in real life. Social media companies might benefit from remaking the overall user experience, creating a healthier relationship for the user.

Interestingly, none of these recommendations requires that social media companies take on the role of arbitrating between truth and falsehood. Social media companies would arguably do better by presenting their users with a more diverse range of material and perspectives, keeping users' attention by engaging their curiosity.

## Systems Thinking and Political Division

Political polarization is increasing around the world. The bitter debate surrounding the United Kingdom's membership in the European Union and the close vote to leave in the 2016 referendum is just one example. Politics in the United States have also become very sharply divided. Significant percentages of both self-identified Democrats and Republicans are inclined to see members of the other party as their enemy, meaning they fear that the election of an administration from another party might mean the end of their way of life.[20]

A complete breakdown of the American political system would be too ambitious for this introduction to systems thinking, but it seems fair to say that at least part of the dynamic is an escalation of conflict between political camps.

Because partisan politics is essentially a zero-sum game, one party's success will come at the other party's expense. Britain will either be in the EU or out of it, and in the US only one party can hold the Presidency, or have a majority in the House of Representatives or the Senate. That basic truth of politics will make this particular cycle of retaliation harder to escape.

Within this escalation cycle is another escalation cycle, if not in reality then at least in the perceptions of partisan activists. Consider that one side believes that elections are marred by fraud while the other believes its opponent is prepared to engage in vote suppression, denying access to the ballot to ensure its victory. It does not help that elections are administered by local officials who themselves are often partisans.

Even if this cycle only happens in the heads of party activists, it accelerates the process of escalation, adding to the perceived threat that comes with a disappointing election result. Partisans of either side can motivate their voters to claim that this election might be the tipping point. Their opponent takes power and then cements itself in power permanently through election skullduggery or censorship, or other methods of repression.

This suggests that one good first step on the way out would be for the parties to unite around election law reforms that address both sides' concerns. Start with a commitment to counting votes from all eligible voters, perhaps through automatic registration. Then match that by putting firm safeguards in place to confirm voter eligibility and prevent "ballot-box stuffing." This would likely mean ensuring representatives of both parties are actively involved in election administration at all levels and all locations.

Leaders of both parties should also remember that while elections may be zero-sum in nature, it is possible in escalation cycles for both parties to lose over the long term. Just as neither Texas Instruments nor Commodore was able to remain in the personal computer market indefinitely after their price war, the beneficiary of out-of-control animosity between our traditional parties might be a radical third party that might gain critical early support by cynically presenting itself as the alternative to the bitter fighting between Blue and Red.

# 8

# Conclusion

In the well-known story of *The Blind Men and the Elephant*, each of the men encounters some part of the animal and comes away with a very different impression from the others. One finds the trunk and thinks it reminds him of a snake. Another wraps his arms around a leg, which reminds him of a tree. A third gets his hands on its rope-like tail, and so on.

It's not that these blind men were fools. None of them were entirely wrong, they described their parts well enough, and one could, in fact, put these together to assemble a decent picture of an elephant. This is the essence of analytical thinking. But there is a whole other way to "see the elephant," and that is to observe an animal in the wild, watch how it moves as part of a herd, see how it relates to others of its kind, what it eats, how it reacts to predators. In many ways, this is a superior way to look at things: you get to not only see how the parts come together but how they move and how the whole elephant behaves.

Systems thinking begins by trying to see the whole elephant and understanding where it fits into its environment instead of breaking it down into its parts. As one sees it move, one notices repeating patterns, causes, and effects that won't be apparent if one focuses entirely on the parts.

Systems thinking encourages curiosity. To better understand how a system works or how it might break down, one needs to be willing to go beyond surface explanations.

The "Five Whys" process of taking every explanation and finding out what lies beyond it can be very useful for getting a fuller understanding of a system's inner workings. As you go through the five whys – turning the last explanation around and asking why *that* happened – you are likely to find that the incident is part of a larger pattern, and that pattern sheds light on the larger system. You may find yourself changing your understanding of how that system works and even developing a vision of a new system.

Systems can take many forms. Some are social systems that are made up of people pursuing common interests. Some are mechanical, or biological, or a mixture of all kinds of things. But systems have important common elements that system thinkers watch for closely. Systems will have feedback: actions and reactions will create causal loops. These feedback loops can serve as a stabilizing mechanism, or they can cause a process to accelerate and gain momentum. Sometimes they can overload a system and cause it to fail.

Systems have hierarchies. The system you are looking at will have subsystems, and will itself be nested in a larger system. As you see the relationships between systems, you will understand the role each part plays.

Systems are synergistic: the sum is greater than the whole of its parts, and the effect of a system is different from the effect of any single part. When a part is taken away, the system will not work, or at least it won't work as well as it did before. This is why you can only learn so much about something by taking it apart. You'll find out what the different pieces look like, which might be helpful, but without the other pieces around them, they won't actually *do* anything.

Above all, systems have a purpose, a role to play that is assigned by either a human designer or by the larger system.

Over the years, system thinkers have developed graphical tools that help them think through systems and explain them to others. Connection charts show which parts of a system influence other parts. Behavior over time graphs allow you to track one variable and see how it varies. Causal loop diagrams highlight feedback that can guide a system toward equilibrium or can cause it to spin out of control. Stock and flow charts show how resources flow through a system.

All of these tools can help you understand how a system works and recognize when a system is failing in its purpose.

We looked at a few feedback patterns that crop up repeatedly. You should become familiar with these patterns, the effects they have, and how to counteract them.

Systems thinking is widely used in businesses, but it can be applied in government, nonprofits, even in relationships. But if you want to apply systems thinking well, it helps to make it a regular practice in your business and your daily life. By returning to it regularly, you learn about the systems and subsystems you deal with and learn to recognize the patterns of feedback. Like all skills, systems thinking takes practice, but learning these skills can change the way you look at the world and help you work more effectively with all the systems surrounding you.

# Thank you

Thank you again for purchasing this book, I hope you have enjoyed it!

If you did enjoy this book, could you leave me a review on Amazon? Just go to your account on Amazon or type the below link in your browser:

https://www.amazon.com/review/create-review?asin=B09RB37617

Thank you so much, it is very much appreciated!

# Notes

## WHAT IS SYSTEMS THINKING?

1    The late Russell Ackoff, a professor at the Wharton School of Business and a pioneer of systems thinking in the US, provided a useful explanation of the distinction. You can see the video here: https://medium.com/everything-new-is-dangerous/the-difference-between-analytical-thinking-and-system-thinking-83c5e8225a7e

## LEARN TO IDENTIFY SYSTEMS

2    Source: Daniel H. Kim, Introduction to Systems Thinking, 1999, p. 4, https://thesystemst hinker.com/introduction-to-systems-thinking/

3    Powell, Russ, Systems Thinking and the Five Whys, Peregrine Performance Group, 2014, available online at https://peregrine.us.com/systems-thinking-the-five-whys/#.YBr0y3l MGCg

4    Gokcen, TJ, Nuclear Disasters and Systems Thinking Part 2/3: Chernobyl. Ukraine, Nov 24, 2020, available online at https://www.linkedin.com/pulse/nuclear-disasters-systems-thinking-part-23-chernobyl-ukraine-gokcen;

The Chernobyl cover-up: Chilling book reveals how Soviets knew for 10 YEARS that the reactor which blew a mile-high plume of radioactive dust across Europe was an accident waiting to happen, The Daily Mail, Feb 16, 2019, available online at https://www.dail ymail.co.uk/news/article-6713109/Chernobyl-cover-Soviets-knew-10-YEARS-reactor-accident-waiting-happen.html;

Potter, William C., Soviet Decision-Making for Chernobyl: An Analysis of System Performance and Policy Change, National Council for Soviet and East European Research, 1990, pp. 5-13, available online at https://www.ucis.pitt.edu/nceeer/1990-802-12-Potter. pdf

## UNDERSTANDING HOW SYSTEMS BEHAVE

5    Kim, Daniel H., Introduction to Systems Thinking, Pegasus Communications, 1999, available online at https://thesystemsthinker.com/introduction-to-systems-thinking/

6    Wolf and Moose Populations, the National Park Service, available online at https://www.n ps.gov/isro/learn/nature/wolf-moose-populations.htm

7    Kim, Daniel, H, Introduction to Systems Thinking, 1999, p. 10-11

8    Systems, Boundaries, and Environments, Future Learn, available online at https://www.fu
     turelearn.com/info/courses/systems-thinking-complexity/0/steps/20374

9    Gerber, John, Systems Thinking Tools:  Understanding Hierarchy, available online at
     https://www.futurelearn.com/info/courses/systems-thinking-complexity/0/steps/203
     74

10   Velikovsky, J.T., available online at https://storyality.wordpress.com/2012/12/11/storyal
     ity-14b-creativity-the-missing-link-between-the-two-cultures/

MAPPING SYSTEMS

11   Kim, Daniel H., Introduction to Systems Thinking, Pegasus Communications, 1999;

     Molloy, Janice, Learning About Connection Circles, Systems Thinker, 2018, available online
     at https://thesystemsthinker.com/learning-about-connection-circles/

COMMON PATTERNS AND HOW TO DEAL WITH THEM

12   Continuous Improvement Associates, Systems Thinking Archetypes (Generic Structures),
     2003, available online at http://www.exponentialimprovement.com/cms/uploads/Arche
     typesGeneric02.pdf;

     Kim, Daniel H., Systems Archetypes I: Diagnosing Systemic Issues and Designing High-
     Leverage Interventions, Pegasus Communications, 2000, available online at https://th
     esystemsthinker.com/systems-archetypes-i-diagnosing-systemic-issues-and-designing-
     interventions/

13   Despair Inc., Procrastination, online at https://despair.com/products/procrastination?
     variant=2457305219

APPLYING SYSTEMS THINKING

14   Kim, Daniel H., Introduction to Systems Thinking, Pegasus Communications, 1999, p. 17

15   Toyota Corp., Toyota Production System, available online https://global.toyota/en/compa
     ny/vision-and-philosophy/production-system/

16   Presidio Graduate School, A Tale of Three Bins, 2012, available online at https://www.sab
     re.com/images/uploads/A_Tale_of_Three_Bins_Sabre_Holdings_Case_Story.pdf

17   Lannon, Colleen, Reforming the Schools: A Systems Thinking Approach, The Systems
     Thinker, 2018, available online at https://thesystemsthinker.com/revitalizing-the-school
     s-a-systems-thinking-approach/

18   Artefact Group, Can Social Be Saved? A Design Approach to Solving for Systems, 2019,
     available online at https://www.artefactgroup.com/wp-content/uploads/2019/01/Can-
     Social-Media-Be-Saved-White-Paper.pdf

19   Artefact Group, Can Social Be Saved? A Design Approach to Solving for Systems, 2019,
     p. 18, available online at https://www.artefactgroup.com/wp-content/uploads/2019/01/

Can-Social-Media-Be-Saved-White-Paper.pdf

20  Most Republicans see Democrats Not as Political Opponents But as Enemies, Washington Post, Feb 10, 2021, available online at https://www.washingtonpost.com/politics/2021/02/10/most-republicans-see-democrats-not-political-opponents-enemies/

# About the Author

Henry M. Burton is a researcher and writer living with his wife and son in Austin, Texas. After graduating with an economics degree he spent most part of a decade living and working across three continents. Burton writes non-fiction with a passion for breaking down complex academic subjects into easy-to-read books and articles.

# Also by Henry M. Burton

**Your First Research Paper - Learn how to start, structure, write and publish a perfect research paper to get the top mark**

https://www.amazon.com/dp/B08ZF9CBP1

In Your First Research Paper, Henry M. Burton provides an easy to follow guide for everyone who has never written a research paper before or who wants to get better results in their next paper.

Made in the USA
Columbia, SC
14 September 2023

22871468R00043